Finding Your Prayer:
Path to Healing and Wholeness

Bella Erakko

*Dedicated to
Hawa
who prays naturally ...
through love*

© 2018 All Rights Reserved
Bella Barbara Erakko

Introduction

One day several years ago, I sat in my favorite green chair, teacup in hand, in that predawn quietness, with my mind wandering here and there. Not surprisingly, it wandered into a quagmire of self doubt. As I felt myself sink into a familiar sense of bleakness, it occurred to me that I didn't have low self esteem in *every* area of my life. Just *some* areas.

This thought brightened me considerably. If, for example, someone hated my writing, it wouldn't bother me much. I enjoy writing; I feel I write reasonably well. But if someone attacked me as a mother, finding fault in the way I raised my children, I would immediately heap "not-good-enough" thoughts upon myself.

Suddenly an image floated into my mind—that of a rowboat, one with a few holes in it. Basically seaworthy, it just needed some bailing. I envisioned one hole for every aspect of my low self esteem. I realized some people might have three holes; others five or nine or eight. *What if,* I wondered, *I created a prayer with one line for every hole in my boat? Then,* I surmised, *I could say that prayer any time I hit the rough waters of <u>my</u> low self esteem.*

I took my journal and began to write. Over the next several days, I came up with an 8-line prayer—my bark had 8 holes in it.

Then I began to pray it, and to my surprise, it helped. Except for one little thing. I couldn't affirm myself *by* myself. I recalled all those self help books that focused on positive thinking—pasting stick-its on mirrors and refrigerator doors. If <u>I</u> tried saying them, I just sank deeper into a sense that I was lying to myself, saying an untruth.

For example, the first line of my prayer was, "I love myself." But when I hit an area of low self esteem, I clearly do *not* love myself, and saying it just lacked power. I was bailing the water leaking into my boat—but the water was coming in faster than I was bailing.

Weeks went by with no solution. I kept hitting this roadblock. Then one day I asked myself, *what if I added the words "in You"?*

"*Who?*" I silently asked myself, *is this "You"*? For me, coming from a Christian tradition, the *You* was God or Jesus or both. But I realized if I were Buddhist, that *You* might be Buddha. If I was drawn to New Age thinking, *You* might be Divine Love.

So I rewrote the prayer, ending every line *in You*. Now my first line read, "I love myself *in You.*" Immediately I felt my heart soften, and open to healing energy.

That happened several years ago. My boat still has holes in it; but I have very good plugs that work pretty fast when I'm "in a situation."

My prayer won't be your prayer, but I hope this small book opens a door for you so you can begin to explore your own rowboat through life. But now, I want to back up and tell the story of my prayer more fully …

My Story

     Why don't we believe in our own goodness? What happens to us that allows us to so adamantly bury every good treasure within ourselves? Why do we become so blind to our beauty—but with x-ray vision see our faults?

     We protect ourselves. With each wound, we take a psychic trowel and plaster over the memory, protecting it with shell-like precision— no lock, no key, no door or window —encase it and hope to forget it forever.

     Some of us encase ourselves in fear; others in rage. We think we are making our life safe and secure by creating a wall between our tender soul and the painful events of life. But as we well know, walls keep everything out—even love. Worse, we forget what we have separated ourselves from—if we ever knew it existed.

How does one crack open such a shell?

I asked an elderly Oklahoma woman one day what it felt like to finally get electricity. After all, she lived for decades in a four-room wood-burning, kerosene-lit stone cabin. "How did you do without it all those years?" She answered simply enough, "You don't miss what you don't know."

She lived on a farm, her "shell" unconnected to the power grid.

A shell keeps you alive. It protects well. It seems impermeable—as though one lived in a cave and didn't know an entrance existed. Not knowing, how does one emerge to see one's shadow upon a grassy meadow on a sunlit day?

When I was young, my shell sealed me away like a prisoner because I felt different. Not fitting in gave me a confused idea about love and belonging. In my fairy-tale imaginings, the unconditional love I craved floated on angel wings but never really touched *me.*

As though I received a wrong wiring schematic, the world didn't make a great deal of sense to me. So while my parents loved me in a way that seemed normal to them, they didn't know how to comprehend my thoughts and emotions.

I suspect that a great majority of us, if we were honest, would admit to similar feelings. None of us are "normal" – we are incredibly unique.

But in a Hallmark-card world geared towards the idyllic, we feel *we* are the Pinocchio's and *everyone else* is real. This may create self-hatred ... or not.

On a mental level, knew this. I felt like the orphan outside the brightly lit store filled with gaiety, loving people, and wonderful treats. I did not succumb to rage—it wasn't lady-like. I buried it. I didn't destroy relationships; I mimed them by action and word, hoping that would make them real —like Pinocchio turning into a *real* little boy.

~ ~ ~

I do believe in longer soul-spans than one single life. I like to believe it because, to my mind, Divine Love invites us to divine love.

How could one life suffice to teach such a lesson? Why not have several lives? Might not "heaven" seep into us, slowly, life after life, until we embody heaven-on-earth? Why wouldn't heaven be everywhere—in every thing, every place, every atom? Then we'd have no choice but to stumble upon a way out of our en-shelled existence. But how? Where? When?

I know how to blame myself for everything. Occasionally I think to cast blame on others, but like a boomerang it flies right back to home port—me. *I'm not good enough.*

None of this, of course, is true. But we have to begin (even while we most emphatically do not believe we are lovable) to chip away at this thick shell. It is our responsibility and no one else's.

I waited a long time before I raised my hand to this shell. I expected romantic love to find and save me. Like a princess imprisoned in a castle, I waited to be rescued from my own faulty thinking. I believed I had done no wrong. I was a stranger in a strange land, unloved and incomprehensible.

But none of us—not one—can solve hatred and fear, abandonment and shame, guilt and self-loathing, by waiting to be rescued. And worse, if we rail and rage righteously throughout this life, we carry these woes right into the next—until we chisel our way out of this protective shell and are truly born into the Love that is ours, and always has been ours.

In my early years, I believed I *was* my actions. I worked in a male-dominated business and I became "man-ish." At that time, I would have believed we are nothing more than an assemblage of cells wrapped around DNA as merely a biological entity.

Our modern culture encourages this disconnect.

We are a people of doers rather than be'ers, yet it only takes a bit of uncomfortable silence to notice the reality: we are trapped in a who-what-when world rather than a deeply relational be-world.

~ ~ ~

Now imagine the child born into families with secrets—the secrets of parents who lived under the secrets of their parents and parent's parents.

We do not truly know the story of our mother or our father. There are always hidden stories. A child cannot shelter herself from hidden stories—they flow into her as though they were hers. She cannot distinguish.

She feels parental issues she cannot understand and believes they are *her* fault. No child remains immune. Each child receives both hidden dark stories, and love. The proportions may vary, but both will be present.

The child takes all of this in—and builds a shell accordingly. If the child feels unsafe, the shell is thick; if safe, more porous. But every child—every human—has a shell.

The child also brings her own story of past lives into the family. Sometimes souls with very different paths can land in the same family. These are not "good" souls or "better" souls or "bad" souls. The Dalai Lama says that any soul born in a human body has great courage—and also great opportunity.

Illness and surgery gave me the opportunity to see the world I had created. I began to grapple with questions I had never before asked myself – why did I live this way—almost running away from my own self?

I began to change my actions. My husband and I adopted two daughters. They became my teachers in the sense that we cannot hide elephants from children.

Sometimes through the pain of my daughters' hidden stories, I began to truly see my hidden story. I tried to become honest—the kind of honesty that makes you admit that you secretly believe you are unworthy of love.

Now how does one affirm one's self out of that? Saying "Mirror, mirror, who is fairest?" does not break an image of such negativity. Within hours, we have cursed ourselves again. "I was late picking up my children ... I'm irresponsible." Like a tide, waves of doubt wash back into our lives.

So, if one feels completely self-contained in such an emotional prison, with no key or window or door or crack in the floor—*how do you get out?*

I can tell you, absolutely, that you can, in this lifetime, reduce self-hatred to a residual memory—one that touches your heart gently to remind you of what you are not. I know without hesitancy I am loved.

For some who have suffered so much, the only Entity that can gently nurture the piercing of the shell is the Divine Love to whom we call when we are desperate.

For some, it is the unformed Energy of Love. We cry out *towards* the Cosmic Force that made us—even though we do not and cannot know it. For some, it is God, Christ, the Holy Spirit, the Trinity, Buddha, Quan Yin, Mary. In the prayer that follows, I call that loving force, *You.*

Often that cry comes at the darkest blackest most hopeless of times. Finally we cease defending ourselves. We stop trying to bury what we believe to be our dark unredeemed side. We simply give up.

So overwhelmed by yet one more burdensome brick upon our towering self-doubt, it collapses and in the rubble, we emotionally come to a standstill.

Christians might call it Advent. In the dark. Waiting. At the bottom, in the crumpled tower of our hurtful self delusion, finally we ask for help—often without even words. We wait. We watch. We insist. We cease raging against ourselves and others and turn our angry angst toward the Loving Force—whatever or whoever that might be. *That is a strong portal into Love.*

We finally raise our arms against the enclosing shell. It breaks into a hairline fissure. The membrane of our soft heart is exposed. The *You* enters. It may be fast; it may be very very slow. It will be safe ...for *you*. At last, you are to know Love. For you *are* love.

~ ~ ~

As I forced my way through my shell, friends tugged on the other side—bluntly pointing out my lies to myself. *They* believed I was *love* before I believed that the prison I lived in could be broken. I took many paths—but the one that holds the sum of my long trek is a prayer than can be spoken in eight sentences.

This prayer, I believe, can hold the hairline crack of hope open. That is its purpose. It touches all wounds, all broken areas. Its purpose is to heal.

I say it to remind my heart of where I've been and where I go. It is my life-map of Love.

Say it one time; say it one hundred times, one thousand times. It symbolizes a *new* shell, one that vibrates with self-compassion, humility, and faith. True, many times I still feel the *soft* wound of self-hatred. They are part of my topography—the inner landscape that formed me as I grew. True, I will never be entirely free. But I respect this force because I walked on a new path set before me into mountainous heights. The beauty of the mountain is to gaze upon the valley, to give gratitude for the strength you had to climb, and to know that you've left the path a bit more trodden for others. You have left *love* upon the trail.

Now I will tell you the prayer.

The Prayer

I love myself in You
I bless myself in You
I accept myself in You

for this reason ...

I take care of myself in You
I trust and protect myself in You
I reveal myself to others through You
I listen to others in You

With Your help, I offer love and compassion

*T*hese are the eight treasures—my secret keys—that helped me to pierce the shell of this low self esteem. We can live for decades with a belief system that seems so absolutely true to us, it is inconceivable that we might be wrong.

The first inkling I had that I lived in a self-imposed prison came one day when I talked to a friend about my life at home. Terribly upset by what she heard, she slammed her hands upon a kitchen table. The sound of her hands hitting that table woke me up.

Writing this today seems strange to me, as though this story belonged to someone else. Yet, at the time, I unconsciously believed I was not lovable—because I felt different. I concealed it very well. I was talented, reasonably attractive, in a long lasting marriage. I went to church. I belonged to a writer's group and published some of my work. In many ways, I was happy. But I didn't believe I was lovable—and marriage had not convinced me.

Perhaps I had set up the wedding contract in such a way that not even a husband could pierce the secret language of my feelings of not being lovable. The subtleties of our ways of covering up shame and guilt are quite sophisticated. No one would ever realize I was anything but confident and capable—fully engaged in life and enjoying it immensely.

But secretly and constantly, I felt overwhelmed by tiny gnat-biting negative thoughts about myself, of which I was completely unconscious until my friend Mary slammed her palms upon the table. She pointed out how often I made self-deprecating remarks. I insisted they were simply the truth. I was no good at certain things. But as she began to repeatedly ask me to stop, I noticed how *often* I expressed myself that way.

From that moment to this, nearly three decades have passed. This prayer did not come to me at the beginning of the journey, but rather towards the end. It summed up every lesson I had to learn.

When I say it, I feel as though I am reminded of how beautiful the journey became as I began to fight for myself and my beauty and the love that I was. In a way, I needed to *find* the prayer.

I often used prayers of repetition. Tiny fragments of words that softened my heart. But this prayer, for me, undoes every wound, heals every pain, promises all hope, and assures me in every way possible that I was created by Love for love, for myself and others.

I love myself in You

One day, a long time ago, when I was lost in guilt and shame, I asked for a prayer I could say. I began to receive the words—self-affirming words. I love myself; I bless myself; I accept myself… but I could not say them. I did *not* love myself; how could I *bless* myself; and I could not *accept* myself either.

Then I was given—"in You"—and that made all the difference.

I placed myself completely into Divine Love. In that safe space, I could peek out like an unfeathered bird. I could say, with belief, these words.

And this is the right relationship, truly. For we *cannot* love ourselves—of ourselves or by ourselves. One cannot love one. I cannot look in the mirror and say, "I love myself." There is the very image I've learned to find fault with—to not trust. *This* is the very "one" who whips the lash at me. It is me!

But when I say, "I love myself in You," everything shifts. It is as though I have gone to this place of safety—the one place in the world where I have experienced the most safety in my life. Perhaps I might remember how I felt holding a newborn infant, feeling unconditional love flow between us, or the memory of a parent or grandparent, teacher or friend, who always made me feel loved. When I say, "in You"—this is as close to God as I come. And in the reflection of that Love for me, I can safely and completely say—I love myself in *You*.

These beginning words are you—the chick trapped inside the protective shell that has utterly imprisoned you for so many years—taking your little fingernail and scratching the inside of the shell. It is your act of belief in yourself; your courage.

You begin. Like a fish swimming in water, you are swimming in Love. Now you have to connect your heart consciousness to this Truth.

You do not yet know what this Love feels like. But there is a faint, ever so faint, remembering. For before you were here, you were spirit. Unencumbered by the burden of human error, not feeling the weight of emotional baggage and suffering, you lived in Love. Though even in spirit world, I am told, some feel this Love more permeably than others. Nevertheless, it is *much better* than what you are feeling now in the guilt and shame. So even this tiny glimmer of Love warming the scratch you have made from your side of the shell begins to save you.

For you *are* being saved from this devastating pain; this terrible misunderstanding that you are unlovable. You are loveable.

I am loved in You.

I bless myself in You

Blessing builds upon love. It amplifies the angelic energy. It is saying—if "A" is true; so must be "B." You are blessing your self. You are seeing yourself as a blessing, as blessed.

When we ask for a blessing, we are asking for goodness to pour into our lives. We are asking for the Gifts of the Spirit. We are aligning ourselves with Hope. And we are counting ourselves worthy of being a blessing, of being blessed by Divine Love.

It is a great commitment.

It is as though the bride tells the groom, I wed thee with all my heart; or the groom tells the bride, I commit myself to thee all my life. Each is blessing the other with their heart.

When I am blessed "in You," I open myself up to utter trust that I will receive the blessings of Divine Love. I will literally be surrounded by this Love, like a fish surrounded by its water-of-life. Blessing is an encompassing energy. It is meant to surround.

Imagine now you are in this egg, this hard-shelled protective barrier. But you have made yet another scratch upon the membrane—and moreover, the shell has a hairline crack.

Into this tiny portal, blessing slowly seeps in. Not in an instant. Again, this is a prayer of one thousand, ten thousand, scratches. It is like you are scratching what seems to be dry dirt, believing an endless spring lies underneath.

This is, in fact, the story of St. Bernadette. She had visions of Mary, Mother of God, in the 1800s.

This illiterate peasant child fell into a trance, and received messages from Mary. Soon crowds of people followed her to the grotto to watch. One day they saw, to their horror, her scratching the dirt like a chicken in a barnyard. Then she took wet mud and stuffed it into her mouth.

Many, convinced she was crazed, left that day believing her insane. But the next morning, a villager walking by saw spring water flowing out of the very spot where she dug, and miraculous healings began to occur.

This is a story to remember when you say, "I bless myself in You." You are like Bernadette, scratching the membrane of your shell. You are love; you are meant for love. This shell is the soil separating you from the endless Spring of Divine Love. You are meant to be bathed in this water, as though soaking in a tub, warm and secure as a baby.

I am blessed in You.

I accept myself in You

Ah, here we finally face our basic dilemma—we believe we are not forgivable.

Even if we ask to be forgiven, in this entrapped state, imprisoned in our little egg, we do not believe we can be accepted—especially by the Source of Divine Love. All of Divine Love curses us because we do not measure up.

But we are already accepted. We were *created*. The deed is done; it took. You cannot deny creation. But, we argue, we are a *bad creation*. Love, however, cannot create badly. It is like beauty attempting to create ugliness.

If it has no ugliness in it, how can it reproduce it? There is a Divine blindness here.

No matter how much you *believe* you are a bad creation, you are not. All you can blame yourself for is making certain decisions that, in hindsight, hurt you and others. You are like a tarnished sterling silver spoon. You are silver nonetheless.

To say "I am accepted in You" is to acknowledge that *you* are much more than your previous actions. In fact, you are much more than the future actions that cast you into feelings of shame and self-hatred again. For you are a human. You are aimed—by this prayer—toward the Light. But of course you will fall flat on your face, again and again.

It is the *direction* in which you are walking—not the success of each step—that allows you to say with utter conviction, "I am accepted in You."

We are human beings. It is very very hard to be a human—so complexly made, so filled with thoughts, emotions, memories, reactions, so fatigued with work and money worries, so wanting to do right and feeling you have missed the mark.

Of all creatures, humans are heroic and courageous in even their *attempts* to be good. Of course, you are accepted.

No human, no matter how seemingly holy, skips along the path of Earth.

If you *live* in acceptance, falling down—making an error in action or judgment—simply means standing up again, making amends as best you can, and continuing the journey in faith. You can learn to *feel* the Light of Love upon you all the time. Yes, it even shines on the shame. The shame hurts. It often causes a stumble. But now there is Light upon it. You see it *in perspective*. You have compassion on yourself. You see yourself as one of millions of other human beings, living and deceased, who also fell often.

They weren't bad. In fact, you have friends. When they error, you feel compassion towards them. You accept them despite this momentary lapse in goodness. You see why they got angry at work, or got the parking ticket.

Often the ones who feel the most shame are the very ones who are most accepting of *others*. This is a strange thing. But it is the one who has fallen often (in their own minds) who are the kindest and most forgiving to others who seem to fall. The righteous ones who feel they've led the straight and narrow good life, do not have this gift of acceptance easily. They often judge and blame and have very little kindness.

So you, who have been entrapped in this shell, *know* acceptance even in your heart. This is not a gift-of-the-mind for you. All that is necessary is for you to *include yourself* in this Circle of Acceptance.

When you accept yourself, you enter into the graces of humility. Perhaps it is impossible to accept yourself, by yourself. But by adding "*in You*," you acknowledge that you are already acceptable. Here you begin to learn humility. For to accept ourselves, we must be humble.

Humility is the opposite of guilt and shame. Humility is finally giving up the belief that you should, by your own bootstraps, create a perfect human life and be a perfect human being.

Measured against that standard, the only possible result is guilt and shame. If you believe *you* are responsible for a perfect world, or at least your portion of it, then you can never be acceptable in your sight.

In the closed world of your egg, one guilt collides into another, one shame swamps another. It feels like a traffic jam!

Acceptance is simply adding traffic lights, paved roads, stop signs, speed limits. Acceptance allows hurtful feelings to flow into and toward Divine Love rather than getting trapped and stuck.

Humility *sees* this inner world in a gracious accepting way. We are limited; we are divine beings encased in limits.

Shame and guilt are born of an arrogance that we can be perfect if we only try. Acceptance comes from a reality check.

To say "I am accepted in You" can fill one with gratitude. In spite of everything I've done—and may do—I am acceptable. And when I look within myself, I now see, and accept, the limits a human lives within in this world. I no longer see myself as a potential god who has failed, but a human who tries, buoyed by Divine Acceptance.

I am accepted in You

I take care of myself in You

Now we turn a corner.

The first three lines of the prayer touch upon the core of our being—our right to exist, to be loved, blessed, and accepted.

They are solitary in that they don't require a *relationship* to other human beings. One could live in a cave, perhaps, and say this prayer endless times. But it does not take into account all the necessities of being—and living—as a human.

When we hate ourselves, we don't take care of ourselves. We endlessly try to escape from ourselves—not even knowing that we do it.

When we feel anxious, we go shopping, binge on food, watch TV, sleep, have sex, get drunk, read a spiritual book, go to church ... again, lash out at others—and *always* say hateful things to ourselves. "I'm such a PIG!" "I'm in debt again." "I got a DWI."

Like an endless mantra, we curse ourselves. It is as though, in our tightly enclosed egg, we use our fingernails—not to scratch our way out, but to claw our own flesh. We wound ourselves.

But if we say, "I take care of myself *in You*"—Oh, then an obligation of loving relationship comes into play. How can I treat myself so badly in the presence of Divine Love. It would be as though Christmas has been robbed of its lights, manger, and angels.

Of course, when we're in the acting of binge eating, or buying that new outfit at the mall, we don't remember to think of these things.

It is not the moment of forgetfulness, but the moment of remembering that is needed.

Like a seesaw, of course we go back and forth. From birth to death. We each have our escape routes. When we feel pain, it is often unconscious in its immediate moments. The pain shifts so fast into our escape route, we almost skip the knowing. Or we *do* know – and the pain is *so intense* we need to anesthetize it.

Either way, we escape!

What causes such pain is relationships. As we try to live in community with others, all of the sudden we are dealing with the *other*—their pain, their shame and guilt. Suddenly, we get wounded—hurt by words or deeds, conscious or utterly unconscious.

If we were to live in utter isolation, never seeing another human being, it would be hard to imagine a way to hurt ourselves.

We wouldn't know shame, because that's relational. Or guilt, because that also requires a relationship. It would be almost impossible to to hate ourselves because we'd have no basis for it—no basis of comparison.

So here we are, wounded by words or deeds, and we react by injuring ourselves. Yet it does not *seem* injurious. Eating a bowl of ice cream makes us happy; having a drink relaxes us. We may even run five miles, not knowing that the endorphins that make us feel good still allow us to escape emotional pain.

To take care of myself "in You" simply holds up the mirror of truth. Every activity mentioned can be good. It nurtures the soul. Even the wonderful glass of wine to go with a good meal, or the beer shared with friends watching a football game. However, in those cases, we are bathed in friendship and love. We are sharing food or time together. Because our bodies are relaxed and in a psychological state of well-being, we take in the ice cream or wine in a grateful way.

But when we feel wounded or hurt, we eat with a sense of inner rage and anger at ourselves. Strangely, the balance is tipped toward self-abuse. We get drunk; we gain weight; we go into debt; we get violent.

"I take care of myself in You" softens the blow. In our little shell, we may witness ourselves doing things to escape a pain ... but we are also hugging ourselves so many times with these words that slowly, like sand going through an hour glass, we temper the experience. There is a softening, a melding, a blending, a maturity. No longer is any *thing* a vice—it is part of a whole, part of who we are, part of love.

I take care of myself in You.

I trust and protect myself in You

We have grown up in an industrialized society. Many of us no longer know how to quickly do simple mathematical calculations. We don't trust ourselves. We hunt out a calculator or adding machine to think for us.

Slowly we've lost our trust in our intuition. We treat it like a vestigial organ—just as doctors consider the appendix and tonsils. They seem somewhat useless, easier to remove than reflect upon their value.

We've taught our children not to trust their gut reaction, partly by not modeling that wisdom. The burden of the scientific era we live in is this: we don't believe what we cannot prove.

Yet, how do you prove "love?" How do you show, under a microscope, that love exists between you and another person?

In our society, we live in a carefully divided world—a parallel universe. In one, everything is rational and explained; in the other, everything is carefully ignored.

Faith, wisdom, intuition, love, life-after-death—all of these fit into the ignored universe. If it weren't for relativity and quantum theory, we would never have found a bridge between the two worlds.

When quantum theory found that a particle—a measurable, viewable "thing"—could become a *wave!* Well, the game was over.

Mysticism garnered game-point advantage but it has taken decades for this miracle of consciousness to settle in.

Perhaps most helpful here is the example of the microwave oven. We stick a piece of meat into this cold box, press some buttons, the box *remains cold* ... and the food cooks. We scratch our heads; we try to understand, quickly give up, and accept it as an essential kitchen appliance.

Some type of ray is vibrating the molecules in the cold lump of raw meat—and it seems like a miracle.

We don't need to know why microwaves work; we trust them to cook our food.

Likewise, to trust and protect yourself means you might not logically be able to explain why a situation or person makes you uncomfortable, but you nevertheless remove yourself. You trust and protect yourself.

We need to re-learn this art of intuition and trust. We have tremendous cellular wisdom in our bodies. It comes from every event we experience. When we are hugged by a loved one, our body relaxes. The cells literally expand. The nervous system smooths out. We breath more slowly and deeply.

Scientists tell us today that our cells have memory. It is as though our brain is no more than a switching station. The real memory resides in the cells, literally bathed in chemicals of love ... or fear.

When bad things happen, our body tenses, our breathing speeds up, we feel anxious, queasy, scared. These reactions may be very very mild—just a sort of "this doesn't feel right."

Early on, we know love from not-love. Abused children instinctively know that what their body is receiving is *not* love. But somehow we fail to trust and protect ourselves.

Another form of abuse is this: to not let our children have their emotions—all of them.

In our culture, even today, when a child comes home hurt, angry, afraid, ashamed, victimized—we often try to distract them.

We almost automatically say, "Don't pay attention to what they say. I love you. You are wonderful. Let's go see a movie."

We teach them how to escape bad feelings. We tell them not to trust and listen to them. Rare and wise is the parent who trusts their own body's wisdom and teaches that to their child.

One mother I know, beginning when her daughter was three, allowed her to learn how to be with hurt feelings. She sat with Elizabeth, asking, "How does this feel *inside* you?"

What a remarkable question! Her tummy might hurt; she might get tight feeling in the chest or a head-ache or back-ache.

Whatever the answer, the mother would ask, "Is it okay to hold this feeling like you hold your pet bunny Thumper?

With Mommy beside her—because Elizabeth felt safe with her beloved rabbit—her mother could ask, "What does this feeling want to tell you?"

As Elizabeth learned to sit with her uncomfortable feeling in an honest trusting caring way, she could give real answers. "I felt left out when Sarah picked Jennie instead of me. Nobody wanted me for the kickball teams. It really feels BAD."

The feeling flows out of its hidden space into the open where a cocoon of love could embrace and circle it. The *feeling* isn't bad—it is honored.

Slowly Elizabeth can decide, together with Mommy, what to do. "I think I'll tell Sarah my feelings were hurt." Or maybe she'll realize, "I'm really NOT good at kickball ... but I AM good at reading."

Rather than being given an escape ("Oh, don't feel bad; let's go out for ice cream.") the child is given a rare treat—the assurance they can—and *should*—listen to their feelings. Over time, Elizabeth will probably learn to listen to *hidden* messages from friends, family, coworkers.

It is important to note that a situation that may hurt one person likely will be of no consequence to another. We react based on past wounds.

When we say, "I *protect* myself in You," we are recognizing that we are not perfect, and in order to feel safe and to grow towards Love, we have to take small steps. If we don't *feel* safe, we become paralyzed and cannot take any step at all.

As adults, we have to regain this innate ability. Our intuition still works, completely intact. Our *connection* to it has become vestigial, like the hidden appendix.

So when we get "the urge" to binge, run, drink, shop—at least we can sit with ourselves and ask the same questions this mother asked her three-year old child. "Where are you carrying this in your body?" "Can you be nice to it—cuddle it, make it feel safe?" "Can you be quiet and listen to the feeling, telling it you really care about it—and respecting that after all these years, it might be afraid of *you*!

Feelings long suppressed are afraid of coming out because we have stuffed them so long into our unconsciousness. But patient effort slowly brings results.

I learned this process as an adult. Known as Focusing—a process created by Dr. Gendlin—it allowed me to stay in a creative positive way with uncomfortable feelings. I well remember my first session: I fell into amnesia.

The trained guide accompanying me had never seen anything like it. I would get to a certain phase and completely blank out.

Not knowing quite what to do, she decided to tell me where I had last "been" in my body. It took weeks before I could even stay with a feeling! But slowly, I learned the inner cartography of my psychic landscape, how I held my wounds, which were deep and which were shallow.

To trust and protect myself, I have to entrust myself to my body—to the wisdom the cells have learned.

Strangely, while I have been taught to literally run away from my body, my body, like a shadow, has always followed me. So its accumulated wisdom has not been lost, only ignored.

It is strange to me how two individuals experiencing perhaps the same event can react entirely differently.

I am not emotionally robust. I am, by nature, sensitive. In my blue collar childhood neighborhood, I was subjected to numerous "inappropriate" experiences from boys and men. Nothing invasive, but enough for my body to *fear* at a cellular level. Now I know how this particular fear feels within me. I can—if I choose—sit with it, comfort it, and promise that I will protect myself as an adult.

These feelings are "golden oldies"—the ones that have very deep roots in my body. Others are less serious.

Someone might say, "Oh, I don't care for your writing." I do not have injuries in this area; my self-esteem never got assaulted. I was able to grow healthily. So my body will *feel* this slight—but it doesn't necessarily need to be attended to as though it were life threatening. It is a scratch-wound as opposed to cancer.

When I pray, "I trust and protect myself in You," I am saying I have an obligation to take care of this sacred body I have been given by the Creator.

I have been entrusted with a great gift—a human body—and it deserves to be trusted, protected, and taken care of. I watch my sacred self in this shell which is slowly softening. I prepare it so it will be ready to live fully when the shell is no longer needed.

I trust and protect myself in You.

I reveal myself to others thru You

When I lived in a world of guilt and shame and self-hatred, I often revealed too much about myself. I had no boundaries. It was as though if "you" knew everything about me *and* didn't hate me, then I didn't need to hate myself. Somehow the other person held all the keys to my kingdom-of-wholeness, and I was the prisoner-beggar asking for freedom from this inner pain.

Of course it never worked. I felt diminished, and even less worthy. Other people wondered, in embarrassment, why I had shared so much. While some friends saw beyond this shame and stayed with me in friendship, others departed.

Now I see this in others who share too much, tell too much, talk as though the silence terrifies them.

When I reveal myself now, it must pass through a filter: *You.*

This "You" is the container of Divine Love, unconditional with only my best interests at stake. If Jesus, Mary, ascended Masters—any of these Divine Lovers—stops me, then I know it is not the right time, place, circumstance to share something deeply personal. The self-revelation need not be told.

The experience of writing this book is channeled through the *You.*

Nevertheless, a healed wound is one that can be revealed, if appropriate to a situation. Its ugliness has a beauty. The scar no longer defaces the humanity of the owner. It only says … "This is a path I have walked upon."

We reveal ourselves in culturally acceptable layers.

First, we offer the essentials, usually name, geographic history, clubs and organizations, professions. Often that will be all that is ever revealed. We level off at socially safe chit chat.

But frequently, the deeply wounded insecure person does not stop there (and often even bypasses this step) to reveal broken marriages, out-of-wedlock children, job loss, affairs of the heart, problems at home.

The pain, so overwhelming, simply overflows the container. The need to reveal comes from a need to pour the pain out onto the shoes of another person—thereby gaining temporary relief.

Such sharing disrespects ourselves. Most listeners immediately have compassion, and see the person in a kind light. But it sets a tone that is unnecessary and damaging.

Intuitively, the listener realizes the person lacks self-esteem. It creates a weak relationship based not upon mutual beauty, but upon a perceived sense of worth—and worthlessness. It is as though a pup has thrown himself on his back, throat exposed—when there is no threat.

It could take many years for the person who reveals too much to see what is happening. Often it is unconscious because self worth is so eroded. But by constantly praying the intention, "I reveal myself to others *through* You," immediately a kind guardian, a loving gatekeeper, has been provided.

"Would I reveal this to a stranger *if* I truly believed I was worthy of love?" Soon, the person tries to withhold just a little bit of the story instead of sharing an entire life. Immediately, the body actually feels *safer*. You have protected yourself. You have valued yourself. You hold your own self with respect. You *have value*. This feels so extraordinary, so surprisingly good, that—when remembered—you soon learn the art of sharing oneself.

When you finally do reveal your story, it comes from a place of self-love, a certainty that you *are* loved and loveable. Then it heals not only yourself, but others.

I reveal myself to others through You.

I listen to others in You

      We have now prayed for oneness of love, for and within ourselves. We have asked for self-care and protection. Now we reach out. We complete the circle. We have received; now we share the gift of love.

      The greatest gift of love we can show is to listen to others with a spiritual intentness. It is as though we fasten one of our ears-of-the-heart to *You*, the divine Creator—and the other to the person we are attending. For the first time, the entire shell that has protected us becomes permeable.

The prayers have dissolved much of the hardness, though the shell still exists—for we still have an ego, and memories, old wounds and scars.

We are now wise. We respect ourselves. But the shell is more like a membrane. It can absorb, with listening kindness, the stories of others.

Often, there is no need to give answers or solutions. We might not know that if we weren't listening through the *You*. This attentive query constantly seeks spiritual guidance. *Am I being called to respond in any way—or to just hold this conversation in quiet love and caring?*

I remember spending a week with a nurse in El Salvador during their civil war when 80,000 people were killed and many tortured.

The death squads especially terrorized the catechists—those who taught the farmers to read and write, those who suggested that Christ had come for the poor and dispossessed.

This nurse lived in a parish in San Salvador. A horrendous earthquake struck the heart of the city. It buried the ramshackle buildings, corrugated roof huts, and a school holding dozens of helpless children.

The entire city was flattened, destroyed beyond recognition. People came to the parish asking for help. She had nothing to give them. No penicillin, no antibiotics, no sterile gauzes, nothing.

She screamed with rage one day to the parish priest, "You should just drive a bull dozer over all of it!"

He gently sat her down. "They just want you to listen."

"Listen!" she hollered, tears streaming down her face. "What good will *that* do?"

He explained, "Listening heals the heart. They need to know they have been heard. Yes, you can do nothing medically—but you can still heal. That is what you must do."

Disbelieving and filled with anger, she nevertheless began to listen. She sat on a wooden backless bench in a cement room in the parish that had not been destroyed. The women and children came. They sat together and told their stories.

When I met her, two years later, while trained teen-aged "health providers" examined the pregnant women in this primitive clinic, she watched over them like a mother over her chicks.

She sat with the older women, sometimes roaring with laughter. Contentment filled the room. Healing had occurred.

If only we would listen with our heart open to God—miracles could happen.

We do not believe that simply listening, without fixing or solving, heals. But we all know of times—maybe just one or two—when we've been heard.

We speak our deepest pain, our horrific fears. We finally *trust*. And someone is there to receive what we say, as sacred and loved. We empty ourselves and find we do not have to pick up all the spoken words and swallow them again. They *could* be gone forever—if we believed the anguished words have been received through this listening person by the Source of Divine Love. Such Love has many many ways to absorb pain—if only we truly understood.

Now, finally, we offer ourselves back. Up to now, we have had to heal ourselves. We have had to re-create a new body, a new temple, based on the Divine *You*. Now we take that *You* with us into daily life, into the many conversations, the chance smiles, the hands held in silence. We listen to the child's story—guiding the child into their hurt with gentle listening love. We become healers.

I listen to others through You.

With Your Help, I offer love and compassion

     What does our heart look like? What has happened to our strong shell with its tiny hairline crack? What has become of the tiny fingernail scratches upon this prison?

     We began with words, repeated one time, ten times, a hundred and a thousand and ten thousand times. The words became our fingernails—slowly determined to crack open the too-protective shell.

Light and Love seeped and then flowed in—slowly and safely so as to not scare us away. At last, there is no need for a shell—not as it once was.

Now the shell is a shelter, a home, a place of refuge, sweetness, and love. It opens; it closes. We choose.

We cannot offer love and compassion based on our own strength or merits. Such things are brittle structures. The ego cannot sustain such "holiness." It could be easy to leave the prayer behind now. We love, bless and accept ourselves now. We take care of ourselves. We trust and protect ourselves. We've learned how to reveal ourselves, and how to listen. In such a beautiful dwelling, anger from self-hatred no longer exists because shame and guilt, while still present, are so bathed in Love, they no longer frighten us.

But now, arrogance *could* surround us. We have succeeded. We have had such courage. We climbed out of the awful pit! We are reborn. We are creatures of Light and Love ... and how easy it would be to forget, in such delights, the *You*.

A healthy ego supports us. It provides a scaffold upon which we, as humans, function in a world of imperfect humanity limited in space and time.

But within us, we now have *wisdom* which functions at a higher vibration than the ego. We *listen* to the *You* and every action flows in and through its energy.

Like an intimate tango, our will melds with *You*—and so it is when we offer love and compassion.

Imagine the ego offering such gifts. Imagine how awry things might go. Quickly, I would want my needs met—I would want to be loved as well as I love. I would want compassion-in-return.

Soon, an internal accounting mechanism would spring up. *Well, I always listen to her when she needs it. But she never has time for me.*

As I go about doing my good deeds, I begin to feel depleted, victimized, overwhelmed. *I am trying to be a good Christian, and faithful to my spiritual journey. I don't say the prayer as often now because I don't need it. After all, I solved all those problems. Now I am the healer! At last, I can give back out of my bounty.*

Slowly the prayer slips away.

Not that our self esteem disappears. It has become a stabilizing force in our lives. But everything feels a bit flat—as though Divine Love only visits once in a while now—when I call upon the *You*.

If, however, the marriage is complete—and we cannot imagine any action without the *You*—then the circle of love spirals deeper within us, and wider outside of us.

We become part of the sacred *Circle-Without-End*.

We offer love and compassion because we have *nothing else* to offer. In the thousands and ten thousand times we have united ourselves to these prayers, they have entered our cells. Now our cells hold the wisdom. Now our cells remember Love. And who can separate Love from each cell? No one.

So we love one another, as we have been loved.

With Your Help, I Offer Love and Compassion.

Amen.

Epilogue

    Over time, I created other prayers — all containing 8 lines. I slowly realized that each prayer seemed especially connected to a different type of need within me.

    I am adding the other prayers here, with the thought that a reader may find one especially appealing, or it might open a path into creating a prayer of one's own.

A Root-Prayer

I use this prayer to literally root myself. The words are ancient and come from two Christian prayers. I literally feel my feet sinking deep into the earth as I say it.

>My Lord and My God
>My Holy One, My Love
>For You alone are the Holy One
>You alone are the Lord
>You alone are the Most High
>Jesus Christ
>With the Holy Spirit
>In the glory of God the Father.

A Prayer of Relationship

This is where I placed the In-You prayer because it truly is the prayer of right relationship. When I find myself in a situation, where I just feel confused or off-center, or angry or depressed, I will say this prayer. It seems to reconnect me to the relationship between my soul and You. I can be present in a more healing way for myself and others.

> I love myself in You
> I bless myself in You
> I accept myself in You
> I take care of myself in You
> I trust and protect myself in You
> I reveal myself to others through You
> I listen to others in You
> With Your help, I offer love and
>   compassion.

A Prayer of Light

This prayer could be for any faith or spirituality. Whether we are Jewish, Christian, Muslim, Buddhist, Hindu or other – all guide us toward the Source of Divine Love. Each of them radiates Light into our world. We choose the Name of the One that most fully opens that felt-sense of Light within us. I often use this one to bless my town. I envision throwing the Light, like a vast net over the sea, across our town embracing all the people starting the day.

> I hold the Light of Christ within.
> I am the Light of Christ within.
> I give the Light of Christ within.
> *You* are the Light of Christ.
> I bow to Divine Love encircling us.
> I bow to Christ guiding us.
> I bow to Spirit/Mother teaching us.
> May we all become as one.

A Prayer of Hope

When I wrote this prayer, some of the lines were enigmas. What is an indwelling mother? Were we the holy womb of life? I have allowed it to remain mystery. It has the cadence of the Rosary, and that rhythm is so ancient and has been said so many trillions of times, it embodies mystery. Saying it this way, with these words, places me in that universal energy.

> Holy Mother,
> Full of Love,
> New creation is within you (or us)
> And blessed is the presence of your compassion.
> Indwelling mother,
> Holy womb of life,
> Nourish us into the oneness of love
> And the mystery of our forgiveness.

A Prayer of Courage

How often are we frozen, unable to speak our truth. This prayer always reassures me when I am frightened to speak or make decisions that are right for me. It takes the burden of the here-and-now and places it in a safer context. All things are passing — even this scary moment. Love never changes.

> Let nothing disturb you.
> Nothing frighten you.
> All things are passing.
> Love never changes.
> Patient endurance
> Attains all things.
> She who knows love wants nothing.
> Alone, Love suffices.
> St. Teresa of Avila

A Prayer of Faith
Each of us has a still quiet place where we feel connected with our higher self, and with the Divine. Here, I bring in a very old personal prayer. For over five years, I lived a deliberate solitary life, exploring silence by living in a suburban hermitage. Each of these words opened a door into a deeper world of Love. Each of us can create a prayer expressing our desire to live Love in our own unique way. This is mine.

>I seek union with God through
>>Silence
>>Solitude
>>Simplicity
>>Solidarity
>>Service
>>and Prayer
>
>That I may love properly.

A Prayer of Gratitude
For me, this prayer symbolizes the juncture between heaven and earth. There are so many things to thank! I have changed this prayer continually as I want to include everything *and* everyone *in this final prayer of blessing. This is the version I use ... today.*

I bow in gratitude to the Mystery of Creation and
To the planets, stars, and galaxies that sustain
    us.
I give thanks to the Masters who illumine us
And the angels and spirit-guides who
    watch over us.
I give thanks to the women and men who work
    with love for peace and justice.
I offer my deepest thanks to all living
    creatures and plants
    animals and plants,
And to the wind, water, rock, sand, and soil,
I give thanks for the gift of gratitude
    and thanksgiving.
        Amen and Amen.

*Making
A
Prayer
Necklace*

Step-by-Step Instructions For Designing Your Own Prayer Necklace

I am a tactile person. As I began praying, I wanted to hold the prayers in my hand. It helped to keep me focused. The instructions below allow you to create your own necklace. Yours can be as simple as knotted string, or as creative as a necklace you can wear as jewelry. Here are the directions for making a prayer necklace:

1. The prayer consists of 8 lines – or 8 beads. To make the necklace long enough to wear, you need multiples of 8's. To separate each set of 8 beads, select a larger

bead. To pray, you would finger each one of the 8 beads with one of the 8 lines of prayer. When you touch the large bead, you would say "Amen" and begin again.
2. You can attach a pendant to the necklace, having a large bead on either side.
3. Any hobby store will carry everything you need. Here is a shopping list:

   a. 20-pound nylon woven thread, non-stretchable
   b. "Big Eye" needle (it has the slit in the middle of the body of the needle)
   c. 40 small beads of the same size that are nice to touch [1]
   d. 7 larger beads for the "Amens"
   e. "seed beads" of a complimentary color in size 10/0
   f. super glue
   g. scissors

4. Pull 40 inches of thread from the spool or cardboard holder. Do not cut off – just

---

[1] The size of the beads will determine how many are needed. You want the necklace to slip over your head without needing to create a clasp, and to have the pendant be where you want it (high or low). Since this is a pattern of 8 beads, you can make as many series of 8 as are needed. This necklace is based on 7mm beads.

secure the spool or holder so no more unravels.
5. Thread one large bead onto the needle and slide onto the thread.
6. Thread 2 seed beads onto the necklace.
7. Thread one small bead (of the 8) onto the needle and slide onto the thread
8. Repeat steps 6 and 7, seven more times.
9. Thread two seed beads – one large bead – two seed beads
10. Repeat five more times until all 40 beads have been used.

<u>Option A</u>: Attaching a pendant
    a. Thread one large bead, several seed beads (enough for pendant to swing freely), and the pendant.
    b. Go to Step 11.

<u>Option B</u>: No pendant
You will end with the 8th bead and two seed beads – and be ready to tie it off, Step 11.

11. Cut excess thread away, leaving about 5" on each end – enough to knot comfortably with your fingers.
12. Gently shake the necklace down. Holding it as though it were tied, slip it over your head. If it is too tight, you will have to add another series of large bead + 8 beads.
13. Tie the two ends together, knotting it three times as tightly as you can.

14. Take the needle and thread a loose end through it.
15. Thread that needle back into as many beads on the left as you can.
16. Remove the needle and thread the remaining loose end through the needle.
17. Thread the needle back into as many beads on the right as you can.
18. Glue the knot well.
19. Pull the knot, if possible, into one of the large beads.
20. Glue the place where each loose thread end comes out.
21. Lay onto a plastic baggy to dry.
22. When fully dry, cut off the loose ends.

You now have a necklace that you can wear as jewelry, and also use for prayer.

NOTES

Made in the USA
Columbia, SC
06 August 2018